"Why can't Jesus / come already? We're a mess." Indeed, *Rodeo* is that brand of backslap—furious and cunning and deftly crafted, by no means reluctant to say the whispered stuff out loud. This book rises above a tough and formidable field simply by not needing to rise at all—the poet's wry and revelatory stanzas ride high through minefields of love and heart-numbing loss before accompanying the reader on, in the poet's own words, a "slow descent into the heart / of the world."

—Patricia Smith, DJPP Judge and author of *Unshuttered*

Sunni Brown Wilkinson's latest collection is fueled by that most harrowing of losses, the death of a child. Remarkably, the resulting pieces are not so much jeremiad as elegy, not so much documentary as hardscrabble celebration. These pages are peopled by neighbors and misfits, strangers and family, and creatured by skunks and badgers and coyotes eating hot dogs behind Conoco. What do these agents have in common? They've figured out how to survive. Over and over, this collection smudges the line between the remarkable and the quotidian. Poets have been singing the West for at least a couple centuries, but not the way Wilkinson does it. Here we have *écriture féminine*, with plenty of room to rewrite the female body via chaps and spurs, Buddha and Wonder Woman, tents and blackberry jam, meteor showers and family trees.

—Lance Larson, author of *Making a Kingdom of It*

Sunni Brown Wilkinson's poetry shines out vulnerable and triumphant, vatic and broken with death and love—and we are naked for all of it. Sometimes tickled by unexpected rhyme, sometimes teased into sinuous rhythm, these poems urge us across the page like daring offerings at the feet of the great Nature we are part of—and that is part of us.

—Annie Finch, author of *Spells: New and Selected Poems*

RODEO

RODEO

Sunni Brown Wilkinson

Winner of the 2024 Donald Justice Prize

AUTUMN HOUSE PRESS

PITTSBURGH

Cover Art: *Learning to Lasso* by Kristin Carver
Book Design: Chiquita Babb
Author Photo: Lyndee Carlston

Library of Congress Cataloging-in-Publication Data
Names: Wilkinson, Sunni Brown, author.
Title: Rodeo / Sunni Brown Wilkinson.
Description: Pittsburgh : Autumn House Press, 2025.
Identifiers: LCCN 2024052489 (print) | LCCN 2024052490 (ebook) | ISBN
   9781637681022 (paperback) | ISBN 9781637681053 (epub)
Subjects: LCGFT: Poetry.
Classification: LCC PS3623.I55334 R63 2025 (print) | LCC PS3623.I55334
   (ebook) | DDC 811/.6--dc23/eng/20241118
LC record available at https://lccn.loc.gov/2024052489
LC ebook record available at https://lccn.loc.gov/2024052490

Printed in the United States on acid-free paper that meets the international standards of
permanent books intended for purchase by libraries.

 Autumn House Press is a nonprofit corporation
whose mission is the publication and promotion
of poetry and other fine literature. The press
gratefully acknowledges support from individual
donors, public and private foundations, and
government agencies. This book was supported,
in part, by the Greater Pittsburgh Arts Council and the Pennsylvania Council on the Arts,
a state agency funded by the Commonwealth of Pennsylvania.

 This book was published in partnership with The Donald Justice
Poetry Prize, part of the Spencer Poetry Awards, which Kean W.
Spencer created in 2005 in honor of his mother, Iris N. Spencer.
The prize recognizes the distinguished American poet, teacher,
and Pulitzer Prizewinner, Donald Justice, one of the finest poets
of the late twentieth century.

CONTENTS

I. Bronc

II. Chaps/Spur

I

Bronc

Being that I flow in grief, the smallest twine may lead me.
—William Shakespeare, *Much Ado About Nothing*

Rodeo

Tonight is a rodeo night, the announcer blaring his bull
and clown doctrine so loud it carries two miles
east to our block, where just now a hummingbird moth
drinks from the pink phlox
with its long wand, and I'm alone
for a moment and the sky
is bleeding itself out over the train tracks
and the abandoned brick factories. The lights
of the carpet store by the mall flicker *carpe,*
and I wonder just what I can seize.
The homeless shelter bearing some saint's name
fills up every night and spills
downtown the next morning,
wings of strange creatures brush our flowers
while we sleep. A hapless moose wanders
a schoolyard before it's caught,
tranquilized. Everyone's looking for it:
a warmth, a softness in the belly, in a bed
of grass. Take it when you can. *Seize it.*

Lately sleep is a myth, and my brain
is so hardwired for worry my whole body
crackles, then a deep fog rolls in and all day
I'm lost. Unlike this moth, greedy in its guzzling,
drinking sweetness without asking,
and now the buzzer of the bull riding sounds.
I think of the grace of that single man,
one hand on the saddle
and the other a flag waving violently
above him—a wild show of surrender.
Some days it's like this: one part
anchored while the other begs for mercy.

And some days it's the other, the posture
he begins with: both hands together, holding tight.
Sometimes you hold your own hand.
That's all there is to take.

Don't Feed the Coyotes

A man stands next to his Harley
            and throws hot dogs
at the mangy thing prowling
            the Conoco. They arc in the air and smack
the concrete and roll a second,
            and the wild dog steps forward
warily. We're on our way
            to Mexico, ten miles past Why,
Arizona, where none of my questions

were answered: Why
did our son   (apple-cheeked, blue-eyed,
                four days shy
                of due)
have to die? Why did I mistake
            the end   for the beginning?
Why is my body
            a decrepit factory, each machine slowly
breaking down? Why can't Jesus
            come already? We're a mess. The world

is a starving coyote,
            and my body the abandoned mine
we passed in Vulture City,
            hardware quiet, rusting. Deep down
a stillness.   My body is that old
            prospector's shack
no one lives in anymore,
            wood dry as kindling in one hundred degrees.

Saguaros raise chunky arms,
        baby-like, Buddhist

monks blessing the cracked
      earth. I love their assurance,
the yoga poses,
      the way they suffer,
hold the good water close,   wait.

Creatures here crouch, desperate
      for life the way a man
haunts a mine on all fours,
      looking down into a hole that will ruin
or save him. The way we did
      that long night in the hospital
after the news. We looked into the hole
of us a long time,   fur matted,
      heads down. Something between prayer
and a baring   of teeth.

We give ourselves
      to what comes
just to stay alive. We read the signs,
      like this one near the Conoco bathroom:
Don't feed the coyotes.

Sometimes a child dies,
      and living things are ugly.
A scavenger begs,
      and in his ugliness,
we see ourselves.
      It's tenderness that makes
Harley man lift his arm,
      for a moment Saguaro-like
but soft, and fling
      that last hot dog
         like a blessing.

They call it weeping

the nurse said as we dabbed the fluid from you, my boy with a birthmark
on your lower forehead between your eyebrows, almost diamond-shaped,
like so many horses I've seen in so many fields. More dark hair than
your brothers and for one moment your eyes were opened—your dad
says *blue*—then closed. Your mouth stayed agape. You were gone before
you came. *I'm sorry*, the doctor said. *There's no way for us to close it.* Not
even breath. Just that open-mouthed awe at your body having made it,
though the rest didn't. Your lips magenta, the color of the succulent's
bloom I smashed between my fingers a month later. Like old bleeding.
Red to purple to black. I held you for three hours, kissed your cold head,
tried to warm you with my breath, but you grew colder and your
tissue-paper skin began to pull away. So much fluid under there. Pink.
And it seeped out like your whole body was crying.

⮑

when, after each morning's bath, my breasts drop
    milk
    tears
    one
    by one
    down
    my
    loose
    and ragged
    torso.

⮑

the kind of willow that loves water

    like the one in the park
where Logan River ran,

where we played
        as kids. A wispiness and the way
even a breath of air
made it flutter.

Like a woman bent over,
        hair brushing the ground,
        riding the waves
of grief
        up and down.

        ∽

what I heard one afternoon
as I walked across campus:
behind the trees
another Mary Magdalene,
hidden,
disembodied
by longing,
some heartache
that couldn't wait
for home.
She released
each guttural note
the way you might hold
a sparrow
against your body,
slowly open your hands and
finally,
mercifully,
let it go.

The Way Things Are Going in Liberty, Utah

The mare in Cook's pasture moves slowly,
      lets the wild turkeys by,
            that parade of angels whose language

is more fuss than cry. In summer we unbonnet
      blackberry stems, drop thumb-sized
            berries into an ice cream pail

in my father's garden that abuts
      Cook's pasture.
            They come easy.

I tried so hard
      to forgive my mother
            for leaving.

Near the house, the roses are heavy
      with the weight of themselves.
            They can hardly keep up

their heads
      until we cut them, take them
            away.

Out in the yard,
      my father cleans
            skunk traps—six skunks

and eight raccoons this month. They come
      in the thick, bottomless night,
            cut through the dark,

graceful as water, surreptitiously
        eat cheese—slippery goodness
                on their claws—then,

the spring,
        the latch.
                The rifle.

Hard to kill, the raccoons
        take three to four bullets,
                and even then, thrash and tear

like a woman on fire,
        like a woman desperate to get out
                of her life.

The skunks, always softer, just spray
        and drop into a heap
                the color of milk and shadows.

They wanted to savor what wouldn't
        last. They wanted sweetness,
                not knowing the other side was loss.

What's the fruit of a whole life?
        And do you wait for it to ripen, or take
                it at will, even steal?

The house is for sale but the garden
        doesn't know it, unstoppable
                in its bruise-colored giving.

Maybe the mare knows best.
        Evening, she dips her head
                into a barrel full of twilight,
                        bobs for stars.

Ghost

All summer my father plays evangelical AM on an old radio in the garden to keep out the deer. Neighbors have barbed wire fences, motion sensors, traps, but he uses singing—the brave hallelujah of being born again keeps them away.

My friend says for weeks a single noisy cricket has sung outside her window every night, kept her awake. One morning she crept out early, poured gasoline on it. Finally, sleep. But no song.

Near the end of June, the baby arrives, but he is dead already. We hold the husk of him in a white blanket before the mortician comes. No blood hum or cry song, just silence.

August moon and stories around the fire, and in the background, my father's radio. We lean in to hear the end of a ghost story   a haunting, a spirit returning home—and from the cornstalks a woman sings "Be Still, My Soul." Crackle of the fire and the spirits we can't see.

"All now mysterious shall be bright at last," we sang near a tiny grave on a June day.

My son is a mystery, a body we held briefly and let go.

My body is a mystery, a cave, a house, a shell.

The Bible says one day the earth will be fire, and we'll all be born again— to singing or to silence. Come to me then, my little deer, my cricket. My darkest hallelujah.

Blackberry Jam

There's a baby in the garden, dimpled
and kicking in the stroller in the shade
that stretches over my friend's yard

like the longest motherly fingers
on an August afternoon.
Out West, we're throat-deep

in smoke, drought. A single rainstorm
all summer, and somehow, there's a wall
of blackberries. We kneel,

reach toward, speak through,
ask, *how was your summer?*
My sons ring the stroller

and gawk, point to the baby's toes,
look how small. Fist as big
as a blackberry.

What we pick and drop
into the old ice cream bucket
is also dimpled, pleated

in a purple violence,
thick as your thumb and muscled.
The blood of it stays

on our hands all day
like Lady Macbeth's, carnage
of berries, the red-telling of ache.

Days later I coax cups of sugar
and pulp into foam on the stove
and the spit from the pot

feels mean and Victorian
in its purse-lipped slap.
I wrangle magma into glass,

that sickly-sweet brew, the sting
of it on my knuckles, up my bare,
freckled arms.

Contained, it's still chaos,
a color that can't make up
its mind: puce of a courtier's

dress, scarlet of Napoleon's cuff.
Cerise, burnt umber,
the deep wine of a baby's lips.

Later, when I unscrew the ring,
hear the pop of the lid,
I'll taste smoke and tang,

the strangeness
of being a woman, alive,
loving every bright thing.

All of history in this jar—
fruit and womb and all
that's spilled after.

Self-Portrait at Twelve

after Kiki Petrosino

Swedish-white, part hush, part bite
Birthed to bury mother's night
Scythe and needle, rake and book
Raised to clean my mother's dark

I am limber, I am strong
I have cut the shadows down

Lapidary finds the stones,
cuts them for my mother's eyes
Sticks and stones and glossy mud
this is what I'm made of

Gone to seed, here's what I bleed in:
moss and marrow, mangled roots,
syncopated Sunday pews,
yarrow, meadowlark and owl

Danish-dark, this hair in braids
Father's left the rabbit dead
Brothers lean on naked trees
I am bleeding at the knees

All day long I trim the tallow
sweep the room and bloom in yellow
dust the portraits of our sorrows
light the candle for tomorrow

I am limber, I am strong
I have cut the shadows down

Someday Soon

He loves his damned old rodeo as much as he loves me.
Someday soon, goin' with him someday soon.
　　　—"Someday Soon" by Ian Tyson, recorded by Judy Collins, 1968

It was the unabashed twang that got me.
Judy too talked like that.
And the moxie in her voice that said,
Blow, you old Blue Northern.

Twenty-one and tough as nails, hanging
on a fencepost waiting for her lover—
to hell with her parents.
When my friend said at sleepovers,

Say hotel, she'd laugh herself to tears
when I said it.
Only years later did I know
it came out *hoe-tail.*

The ranchers and farmers
in my blood stuck
to my tongue too. Southern Idaho
to northern Utah, rocky lands

still dotted with old barns
and dilapidated fences. Like Judy,
I couldn't hide my hick.
She had long brown hair

and blue eyes.
At ten, I had long brown hair
and blue eyes. Someday soon,
someone was coming for me too.

Judy crooned in the front room,
and I parted the brown curtains
of my mother's hair every morning
and she brushed mine, as sunlight turned

our 1970s rambler deep gold.
Somehow, there were horses
on the edges of everything,
and their manes were long

and silky brown too. The world
was a rodeo, and someone
would take me
into the heart of it.

Like Judy, I had to be tough.
He'd be handsome,
that'd help. We'd ride
dusty roads and rope

every dark cloud, our love wild
as a windstorm.
I'll have to leave you
I told my brothers, a secret message

in my goodnight
at the foot of their bunk beds
or in the careful pull of raspberries
from their stems in the garden

or in my brave wading
across Logan River
summer afternoons in the canyon,
for a moment all alone

in the rushing waters.
Someday, I'll leave you.
I'd cry thinking of it, but
each day was a slow goodbye

to the phlox and the poppies,
to the house with its spiders
and stuffed cupboards, to my parents,
still young and not yet uneven

in their love. *Someday soon,*
my ten-year-old heart sang
in 1987, an unending stretch of blue,
and all the windows of my heart blown open.

Canning Tomatoes, Late August

The West is burning,
Yosemite in ash,

smoke choking
blue sky,

and all afternoon I've cleaned
jars, rim and round

bellies stuffed in mounds
of fleshy fires

the garden ignited
under green.

They'll burn bright
in soups

all winter,
in sauces that splatter

my boys' mouths,
ruby smacked

and long stained.
But now at the counter

they're museum,
the freak exhibit:

one hundred hearts
packed, puzzle-like,

swollen tongues
of summer

severed,
apothecary charms

from a century
of plagues.

If I cut out
the breast

of the robin,
would it look

like this?
Pitched

crimson of poppies,
the shape and sheen

of bloody knuckles
of street fighters,

tucked and quivering?
Or the rooftops

of Salzburg
whose castle's

torture chamber
made us shiver,

all that scarlet
hidden

between the floorboards
and masks,

cardinal sins
loud with telling.

How macabre
for such lightness!

I'll confess
this:

I'm sick
with love for the rust

of each globe,
the way I cut

and plunge them
into jars the way

my mother did
when I was young

and she was happy
the first time

and the garden
said

yes

in red
red red.

Grief Sestina

I met a woman who'd been struck by lightning.
She held herself like a firefly
when she told me. That's something,
I thought. She was now her own gold.
I was pregnant then, fourth boy, more full moon
than ever. But all that beautiful milk

went sour when he died, the stuttering milk
that dripped from me, lightening
each day, and by the time the moon
waned, so had I. What came out next was fire,
and like a wild man digging for gold,
you searched for me nights I left something

cold out for dinner, turned some thin
line into a stone wall. Love, drink this milk
of our grief with me, tell me the days are gold,
and though I push you away, let the lightning
of you find the dry tree of me, and after, fireflies
rise from our bed, strike dumb the brutish moon.

Forget the hospital machine blank as the moon
behind clouds the night we turned into something
we couldn't name. Let's reclaim the days of first fire
when in our house of futons and cheap milk,
we rang each other like bells, like strands of lightning.
Love, how the river of you washed me. Oh, the gold

in your beard then and the gold
in the finches winging endlessly against the moons
of our windows. I come humbly in the lightning
of my grief now. I eat the cold crumbs of something

we made together and lost, the chipped glass of milk
rattling in my hands burns me like the longest fire.

This simple meal of our life, more fire
than water in our fractured bodies. Love, stuff gold
into the hands of strangers, spill the milk
of your laughter, anchor the moon
in your quiet hands and give me something
to believe in again. Even a dogged, tenuous light.

And say it: We've been struck by lightning,
that milky gold something
that's changed us, made us strange. The moon on fire.

Conversations with the Dead

The stars are the remains
of the words. Look

how they too are left in the dark
to shine, everything we've said,

all saliva and tears
and whatever rose

like a bubble with our ache
those nights we hollered

inside the heart
of the dark. And tonight

under the meteor shower,
messages come to me

from the other side. My dead son
talks in the tail

of each streak of light, saying,
Tell him you're sorry,

keep buying chocolate milk,
I'm happy. All day,

I open and close like a lid,
all day like a mouth

that can't stop wanting and knows
the wanting hurts.

But under Perseids
it's safe

to lift the weight
over my head,

to telegraph
my graphic grief,

let it stay in that space
we call space

where I can't touch it
or take it back.

Only look and say
I said that. I meant it too.

And tonight
the slow burn

of my words
is answered:

light
like laughter

plunging
toward me.

April 23, 2020, and Today Is Shakespeare's Birthday

and it's raining, a grand gray opening
to the day, the bucolic

dramas unfolding in the grass,
in the nest, in our own humming houses.

Another friend's heart broken, and star-
crossed trees throw their white confetti

over the budding peonies. All of us
are masked now, playing a part, not quite

sure of our lines but the rhythm,
like our heartbeats, leads us on.

All the world's a stage and the play
must go on despite fresh graves,

all the Yoricks we have loved,
the great monologue of death

rolling through the evening news,
armies of us lurching

to Home Depot, lost but gathering seeds,
flowers, like Ophelia: daisies for innocence

we've lost, violets for our faithfulness
in dark times, rosemary

for remembrance
of what we once were, still want to be.

At the throne, our own mad king,
a Lear still loving the wrong daughters,

the crude, threatening tirades, and yet
life is still

a miracle. Here on my lawn
quail chase through wet grass.

Rock cress flaunts its yellow stockings.
Mourning doves sing life's a tragedy,

but all day long, the swallows
peer in our windows, and we laugh

with our children again,
pet the dog all day long.

The fog moves in and the rain falls,
a curtain on a play

we're still naming. If we're lucky,
this one's about redemption.

We Drew Out the Feeble Language

Vienna in August and we walked
Klimt to Mozart, drank
Wiener wasser, a phrase that made our odd

American hearts laugh,
ate roasted chicken
at the Landtmann, Freud's favorite café,

bought a painting of the cityscape
under a storm, napped
in a park until the sun

went down, and walked
to a church bench to sit.
Still—

the city was a mouth
of ivory statues and red carpets,
a language of splendor

we were not born to.
Then, from a chain-link fence
like every chain-link fence,

a family in burqas, black button-up shirts
waved in the streetlight.
They beckoned—that oldest gesture

of welcome—held up teacups.
Refugee floated like a cloud
above them, the way *Tourist* hovered

above us. They offered us tea
and pieces of English and their faces,
bright as stars

in the spacious night.
They offered themselves and we drank
each other's company.

Then foolishly, foolishly,
we drew out the feeble language
of American money. A language

they did not know
or need. It was not bread
or tea. It was not friendship

though we held out our hands.
I have told and retold this story
like I'm picking apart

a knot, trying to find the center,
what's tangled where.
There were no clouds, no words

in the air. We were all reaching
and broken and utterly
human. And like the bright, wise doves

roosting in the city, they cooed,
then gazed,
then turned away.

Envy

Early this morning, mid-December,
when all the predawn creatures
hunt and cry and patter their delicate feet
in snow and every breathing thing
leaves ghosts behind them in the air,
I heard an owl outside the kitchen window,
winged and cloaked in velvety dark
while I sat dumbly at my desk.
All day a small grief has not ceased
to chafe my heart.

So Long

On the road that opens
to mountains and snow,
away from the houses cramped
in their quarters like too many socks
in a drawer, the eye of the eye
inside of me opens.

All the years of children
I loved and feared
would kill me.
Not their brightness
or the electric thrill of their skin
next to mine, not even the crying
that pried me from sleep
but the dormancy of a wild
inner life I loved and knew well.
To survive, it left me. I cared then

for other wild things. Now in silence
it's returning. I turn a corner
to a doe and two fawns. *I know you. I too*
live like this. The body
and the spirit are a bicycle
you ride carefully
and uphill
and for how long?

II

Chaps/Spur

My work is loving the world.
—Mary Oliver, "Messenger"

Poem After Ravel's *Daphnis et Chloé:*
Lent (chiffre 156) Peu à Peu

Little by little the birds of paradise
          wake up,

ruffle their papyrus-
          thin and polychromatic
feathers,   nuzzle

        breast to breast, trill
               into the light
        that breaks

like water   poured
        into a pool stilled
by stars.

        Now the day
        opens and,   exultant and fluid,
            the birds take over
               the sky.

Fig and bergamot.
        Sweet lemon tree.
            The impossible jewels
                 inside
        and the birds coming.

There are lovers here,
        their bodies like rivers,
        like waterfalls.

Lovers like an altar   burning
        so predictably, their bodies

thin and wingless,
      about to be broken.

I don't want another love story.
I want immortality   like this, beaked

and hungry, shucking
      the fibrous shell of us,

the husk torn loose
      and the seed   glimmering.

Snow and Mud and Animal Bones

strewn across the canal road:
early light, absence.
Another morning walk, and the fog
hangs around the mountains
like an absurd dress,
and it's the day after Christmas.
The fanfare is gone and, in its place,
this—

Behind the football field,
the body of some creature
drowned at the mouth
of the drainage pipe.

Gently with my foot I lift
the wet leaf pressed like a shroud
over his face. A recent death,
the body like a sponge,
sopped and flung.

How like a child he is,
limp and innocent
in sleep.

I feel a strange story surface
in the quiet air.
It is the only thing awake
though everything is breathing.
And the earth—siphoned
of color, of movement—
watches to see
if I'll hear it.

I try. I'm trying.

～

Some dream of earth
unfolds
above the blank eyes of the drowned.
It follows me the whole canal road.
I smell it in the air.

I text photos of the animal
to my husband.
Badger, he says. One paw
gnawed off.
Stricken, I think.
The matted fur still looks soft.

I want to nurture the world,
but I'm afraid of it.

～

Prayer is like this: An animal
flattened, a language
we can barely hear.

I try. I'm trying.

The hardest thing to do is listen
to our own story.

～

Even when I was young
a deep logic taught me
I will live forever
but first

I'll suffer,
cry out,
die.

Like that compass
inside me that read
father when I was happy,
mother when I was sad.

⤸

I'm not far from being
animal
or child
or bones
on this long road
where no one comes
until spring.

I have walked like this
all my life, slow descent into the heart
of the world.

⤸

Today, the sky's tongue
is telling fables—
Tomorrow, I'll wake up
a badger,
three-footed and surly,
I'll wander the foothills
smelling fog and dirt.
My bones
will be the size of a child's,
but my heart

will be ancient
and I'll open my mouth
and cry—
a world of spirit
listening.

Ode to the Skunk Who Lives in the Woodpile I Pass on My Morning Walk

Little Sister, you are like the Spirit
Jesus says is like the wind. You come
and are hidden
and leave a stirring in your wake.
You disturb the mind. You are
so close to the earth
we have not yet earned the gift
of seeing you. All summer
you have hidden
in the fragments of someone's
ramshackle cabin, but now
it is October, and I wonder
where will you go:
Who will smell your perfume
and love you again
like I have?
Who will watch your slick shape,
your feathery tail, dip
into the bare trees an hour
before dawn?
Your body is from the age old
black-and-white stages of history.
You are elegant as the silver screen
and as remote. Greta Garbo
of the neighborhood, you slip
into evening's gray gown,
and saunter down to the little farm
where the fat black pig lies
all night in the mud. You are
otherworldly and silent,

sniffling out beetles
and spiders while the moon
slowly rises, like your bright wet nose,
over my house.

Jenny's Slot Canyon, Evening, Late November

for Sean

These desert canyon walls are black from years
of rain. The water paints it so and stains
the varnish dark, a kind of anguish we
weren't here to see. This place a ribcage, slick
and tight, each wave of rock a rung to climb,
a foothold carved from wind's fine blade. We too
are wild and honeycombed, the fissures deep
inside us know too well the pains of age.
In this monastic space, where light and dust
conspire and ruminate, we face ourselves,
our bodies brittle, tinged with slow decay.
But in the winter light, in day's last rays
of gold, our sons are bright and manifold.
We'll tell our love until the telling's old.

Ring

It came in stages.
First—
      a disk barely touching
      another disk.
Coal covering gold
      in slo-mo.
We held ourselves
      in the cold morning air
and watched the sky
      while the forces
that bring us light
        collided.

My husband came shyly
      to the door of me.
But he moved
      with such patience
he was part of me
      before I knew it.
And love, it came   in phases.

Marriage being slow,
      expanding like an empire,
peopled and strange.
      And we, like Egyptian gods
seated and regal
      with our animal heads
        and eternal staffs
watching over time,
      the keepers of our sons.

Later—
      the outline of a cat's head,
      someone said,
a crescent up top
      like ears,
an embrace
      of two plates
stacked
      like dishes,
like
      the slow lean into the orbit
of another.

And finally—
      this:
          eclipse.

Two faces
      in a long gaze
and yes,   everlastingly,
    fire.

Valentine for the Great Salt Lake

From the sky, your clusters of brine shrimp eggs
        huddle and drift into thick brown swirls
                like pools of chocolate milk. You, mother
to millions, amniotic sac waiting to hatch
        innumerable legs, flat and upright,
                that paddle and push tiny boats
of creatures toward each other.
        You are buoyancy of bodies
                toppled with light. You are love potion.

From the sky you are the brightest glint,
        shine of a gum wrapper, a wild lick
                across our desert face. From the sky you are
a lost child. I bring my children to you
        and something primordial breathes
                under our feet. My sons wear
your salty crust, your brush
        of mineral across their bare and freckled legs
                all the long drive home. They sleep inside

your mottled and endless light.
        You are the place
                that held me while I listened
to the meadowlark's song
        on a spring afternoon so wide
                and long that nothing but the wind
in the brown grass,
        and that single bird
                moved. You are the heart of stillness,
heart of lark and coyote, pink heart

of Floyd, the flamingo who fled
the Salt Lake aviary and lived
in the heart of you
for years, migrating then returning.

The sight of him: a flash
of fuchsia, a thump in the chest,
a one-legged valentine
lost in blue.

Tent

Uinta Mountains

How like a greenhouse
peaked and built thin
against the cool air
where rain falls all night
in this place rich
with mountains;
but inside—
almost tropical,
a hothouse of bodies,
the musty scent of us
ripe and earthy,
dirt in our toes,
breaths of our sleeping sons
rise and grow long,
even tendriled,
and on each cheek blooms
a single
pink
peony.

Alaskan Abecedarian

Arctic terns pecked the heads of us Temsco girls till we
     bled, and Jenny wore a helmet to ward them off.
Crush of tourists we turned into boots, jackets,
     delivered them, baptized in slick winter gear—
elephantine—to the helicopters waiting to carry them over
     fields of fireweed, those six-foot spines of flame, to
glaciers. From the air, the ocean, sky, and mountains made
     hemorrhages of blue, and the cavernous azure
ice leaked into lakes. The night we skinny-dipped in it—
     jolt to the core—then huddled around the fire
kicking driftwood into the heat, I
     lived deeper in my bones than I had before, and when
Maddie asked our biggest fear before we fell asleep under
     noonday light at 2 a.m., I finally
opened the door: that God in his eccentric
     panoply of creatures had forgotten my face,
quiet desperation of my breath. But in the morning,
     rising to endless light and water, I heard again the
sound a soul makes when it's filled, a gentle
     tenor in the blood. It came and came in
unlikely ways, like the day my favorite pilot called each view
     vignette of blue or green, told me in his twenties he
worked in Hollywood, built the set for
     Xanadu, that film where Olivia Newton John, forever
young and free, roller skates into ecstasy. Like a wild
     zephyr, love comes to her. And me. And me.

The Year We Considered Foster Care

*Consider how some of these character traits are demonstrated in your
own family—and what you might do to further develop them.*

—email from Utah Foster Care

i.

Willing to help not just a child,   but that child's family

In spring, in the new house, we study   the yard, then
            take down the evergreen,   harbinger of needles
                        and shadows. Curtains of green   falling.
                                    Then, sunlight   soil.

ii.

Able to offer love without expecting it   in return

I plant lavender, coral bells,   impatiens, butterfly bushes.
Late start—new roof, nails, shingles—   so I delayed, but
                                    I'm trying.
            10 bags soil prep
            16-16-16 fertilizer
            $240 at Lomond View Nursery
            Carpathian harebell,   Japanese maple, baby's breath
            Every gift from Mother's Day
                        Mud   on my knees, between   my toes, my breasts,
                        when I remove   my bra—sweat-soaked
                                    and yellowed—to bathe.
                        But—

iii.

Don't take the child's misbehavior   *personally*

March	pandemic
April	earthquake
May–August	drought
September	high-desert hurricane
Whatever rises thrives	for a week, maybe two, then

withers. Soon, we're back
to blank dirt, the wind and heat having licked
all moisture   from the earth.

iv.

Have no expectations. Children have their own path and a right
        to determine   *who they will become*

In July, leaving a summit,   my friend and I find an owl
        on the ground   disguised as a pine cone.
            I nearly step   on it.
                Owl,   we say.   *Baby owl,*
and it opens its mouth to mewl   when we get close.
        Ragged wing,   and we wing   under it a napkin,
        head to wildlife rehab. The owl's tucked   into itself,
tiny storm   of gold and dirt, twig and wood.
When we stroke it, its mouth gapes, snake-
        like minus the fangs.   I'm oddly afraid.
There, we step   from the car and
        the owl   flies off.   Not hurt but
fledgling. The volunteer says   *not owl but*
                poorwill
flies into a grove of oaks   away from hands, and
for the rest of the day   I think, puzzled, *poorwill.*

Poorwill. Poorwill.

V.

Able to make and keep commitments
Being committed to helping   a child is more important
than loving the child.

Early fall   and my sons and I kneel
in a country of dirt, dig seventy-four craters six inches
deep, drop a pale light wrapped in husky skin in
each.   It's a faith   six months long. I tell
my six-year-old   *trowel, not digger*   *tulip,*
not onion.   He claims a spot and plants
a cup,   waters it.   Wears mud
on his lips,   cheek, hair   until bath time.   His face
impossibly beautiful.   No one can take him   away.
My heart   is a cage. I want   what stays.
He says, *I'll water my mud plant every day.* I know and don't know
if he knows
nothing will ever grow there   but mud.

vi.

Have a good sense   of humor.

October, grasshoppers devour   new blood leaves
on the Japanese maple.   I flick one from a stem
too hard   and it bleeds itself out
on the front porch.   I feel guilty   for two days.
Just trying to save   what's finally growing.   So many risks
to harm.   Nearly everything I've planted
has died.   My six-year-old digs up the cup, shrugs
at the nothing that's surfaced.
Can I just play with the mud? he asks.
He likes the sucking sound   of the cup   as it sinks
and rises
sinks   and rises.

Letter to Josie Bassett Morris

Wild West cattle rustler and rancher at Cub Creek, just outside what is
now Dinosaur National Monument, Uintah County, Utah. The cabin
she built and lived in from 1913–1963 is now a historic site.

How long can you woo the blank face
of cattle?

How does your own voice caress
the stretch of 160 acres,

all those drawn-out talks with coreopsis,
poppies, cosmos as wide-mouthed

and electric as the night sky
riding over dust and dinosaur bones?

Wonder Woman of the West,
you homesteaded alone

over fifty years, divorced four husbands,
the fifth's death still suspicious.

For you, Prohibition was business:
apricot brandy and chokecherry wine,

long vine of men twisting
around your door, even Butch Cassidy,

that sagebrush pirate and your sometime
kick-off-the-boots lover,

hiding out in your shade.
Peppery old lady, bumblebee,

bobcat in an apron,
mud on your boots and bruises

on your knees, did you still keep
a shotgun near the door

when you were eighty,
arms muscled but a little shaky?

Years of splitting the lips
of timber or wrangling joint

and spoke into the crook
of fence posts, like the scientists

down the road slowly reassembling
each tree-length bone

of Utahraptor, Allosaurus.
The windows in your cabin

are the bright squares
of a pillbox, that tidy

and tight. Where are the braided
rugs now, delicate as tropical fish

sleeping on the ocean floor?
Your sea was dust,

your ship this tiny log cabin.
Could you smell spring

before it came in the long bend of cloud
and the storm of sparrows? Your bed

of thyme and rosemary like the brightness
of your babies' faces,

wild juniper and pinyon pine
the spices of your air.

Sometimes it feels good
to let the world pass you by,

to open your door,
and there's nothing but sky.

Mother of mud, of steaming pies
of cow shit, of herbs delicate

as a newborn's wrist, I've come
to the temple

of your home
and left nothing but footprints

and this poem, a contract
to apprentice your ghost.

Buddha Has Returned

from his noble and eternal journey
in the form of my friend's mother.
Buddha eats street tacos for her birthday
and laughs a long, hard laugh
at her son's jokes and lets her grandson
tussle her hair. Buddha has borne
three children and watched her body
fall like slow glacier melt.
Buddha shops Target in old blue jeans,
her rear a square that somehow smiles
as she leans over the cart to drop in
a set of cotton sheets while talking
to her daughter on the phone. Buddha grows
hollyhocks and makes flower dolls
for her granddaughters. She taught
high school history for twenty-five years
and remembers the name
of every European city
she's ever visited. Buddha buried
her first husband. Then, her second.
She takes care
of her special needs brother, scolds him
in his tantrums, laughs at his pants
around his ankles in the driveway,
tucks him into bed, though, like her,
he is old. He teaches
patience, cries his wisdom each night.
He might be Confucius.
Tuesdays, Buddha and Confucius argue
and walk the grocery aisles in white sneakers,
two enlightened spirits searching
for frozen corn.

Last summer, Buddha rode a ship into Antarctica.
She stood at the bow and let the breeze
chill even the roots of her hair.
Before her, Buddha saw a garden of ice
always in bloom. She knew the ancient birds
circling the sea and loved them. She held herself close
because everyone who once did that
is gone. Buddha will empty her beautiful
grievances like gifts before she departs again.
She has worn gray like a crown.
She has worn lips like two happy, fat lizards.
She has worn grief into belly laughter.
She gathers the world the way she gathers
her grandchildren
to her bosom and squeezes.
Each time she enters the room,
her wide mouth smiling,
a voice inside us cries
a light, a light!

Everywhere I Look I See a Rodeo

White bulls and a crowd of blue jeans
is the sky today.

Purple yellow pink horses
riding the wind are the wild show
of tulips in our garden. Calf
with his legs tied
is a tulip bulb. Red sash
of cowboys, a poppy.
Announcer: the bumblebee
in a foxglove tube.

The clown hiding in his barrel
lathered in lipstick,
smile wide as a half-moon,
blond wig and bright pantaloons
is your heart
peering out now and then
to tell a joke
and run.

Chasing the bull, his horns
big as myth,
his hooves
making music
is called riding a poem.

Everywhere I look I see
a rodeo.

I love the world like the buster's hand
loves the horn of the saddle,

white mountains of his knuckles
trembling.

It loves me back like pink
jewel-studded hats, swish
of polyester pants, soft shadows
of leather fringe. It loves me
like snow cones cotton candy
churros nachos burgers dogs.
It loves me like a kid
loves his fingers, licks
each one long, grease
stain on his knee.

I fight grief the way the bronco
bucks that wily man on his back,
the arc of those spasms
a kind of prayer.

Like the calf roped and tumbling
I too lie limp at the end
of all things. I am spurred,
wrangled, rounded
up, hog-
tied by the holy.

Everywhere I look
I see
a rodeo.

Love, the cowboy's kid gloves
limp and crisscrossed
over the horse's back
are the two of us, on a Saturday
morning.

At night we chase our boys
down to bed,
hover over them, wild
things we've caught,
their breathing the rhythm
of hooves,
their falling eyelids
parachutes dropping down
soundlessly
just before the arena
lights pop on.

I Drive Past the Cemetery

wrapped in ordinary days.
Like a bird in a nest
you're there: wild and airy
not buried so much as hovering

somewhere between the leaves
of the oak that's grown six feet
since we said goodbye to you.
O, little cloud, little lark

I drive past you longing for you
but tethered to the world.
I'm tapping on my steering wheel
to "Sweet Thing." *It's me, I'm dynamite*

and I don't know why. Or gently swaying
my whole body like some mystic to
"My Sweet Lord." You know I love songs
with the word sweet in the title like

a prayer to tenderness.
I drive past with mountains of brown
paper bags from WinCo, inside:
buttermilk bread soft

as a baby's foot, toothpaste tubes
with Star Wars and cartoons,
strawberries and blueberries huddled
in their plastic cases,

their faces plump and eager.
I drive past Tuesday and Thursday

late morning after class when I feel
so bright alive

after long talks about Chekov
and that cherry orchard,
after undergrad epiphanies and acne,
and the day that quiet student in the back

said, *I saw my first play*
last night it was so good
like her whole world just started
and she knew it.

I drive past with your dad
and brothers from Grandma Jo Jo's
Sunday dinners, smell of her roast
steeped in our clothes, bowl of leftover

salad on my lap, all of us laughing
at your dad's Chewbacca impersonation.
I drive past riddled
with appointments, bad radio, roadkill,

the kilt of that guy who walks
to the tech school.
You love him for that too
you who are bodiless but watch

from somewhere in the trees what bodies do
all day with the current of their blood
like electricity that never shuts off.
O, tiny god with a tiny rose mouth

invisible to me now, we love
the world together: me with my aging tired

wired singing breakable body
and you without yours, watching me pass

your kingdom of quiet, my whole life aflutter
with color and noise and smells, your world
this mystery I lean into for a moment.
Every day I wave to you with my breath

and my heart and you wave back—a breeze
through oak leaves. Above them
even the clouds in their amorphous
shapes play our game:

here a horse running toward
another horse or there a hand,
for one moment, holding
another hand.

Teapot Lake on the Head of a Pin

Today is ancient. The same north wind
that blew over our ancestors
blows over me, all of us foraging

in the thick bottoms of summer
or fishing for brookies
by a lake late afternoon.

The mountains have barely
changed their faces
in a thousand years. Osprey nests

ring the lake from the tops
of pine trees the way they did
the day Caesar died.

And my sons in camp chairs
are nearly prostrate
over books

like some lost painting
by Renoir. Today
is a still life. I eat a peach

in the lavish silence. There are bears
backstage. Their shadows touch
the edges of our minds. Their breath

is the breath of the gods.
And we're common, almost nameless,
dazed

by a day of sunshine and wind.
My husband, fishing from the kayak,
is an island of grace, a drifting red

dance between water and air,
one bright comma in a long sentence
of lake.

Ask me who I'll be
tomorrow. Ask me if I love
the world. Then watch the oar

endlessly break
through a darkness
it cannot change.

What We Did at the End of the World

We played charades to words we'd forgotten. We made a fire of them with our hands.
We wrote songs on the piano, gave them names like "Fox and Mouse" and
    "Lightning Chase."
We watched our parakeets dance in front of their tiny yellow-framed mirror.
We watched them sleep, three on a perch, their quick beaks tucked in.
We made bread. The top cracked open, and we peeled it back and spread butter on
and ate it. We didn't wear shoes. We wrapped ourselves in scarves.
We opened birthday cards to listen to the music hiding
behind the plastic button. We opened and closed, opened and closed until the
    songs grew tinny.
We gathered snail shells from the garden. Forty-seven. We saw one naked at the
    base of the daisies.
We made music with ice and water and glasses. We hummed under the covers
    at night.
We waved tree branches like arms. We waved at the stars. We waved at our
    silent neighbors.
We taped song lyrics to doors. We swept the fuzz from the rugs
into piles of gray hair. We lifted them carefully when they huddled together like
    a nest.
We listened at the door of an uncracked egg.
We watched the quail scurry across the street, that one feather on their heads
    quivering
in the wind like the feathers of great ladies in the movies we watched at night.
We dreamed of the sea untangling its wide blue braids.
We opened our mouths in the morning and salt leaked out.
We called each other *dear* and laughed at words like *rudbeckia*. We planted
rudbeckia. We danced like it. We wore yellow too.
Just before we flew away, we were mirrors. That deep. That true.

When It Comes

For the thing which I greatly feared is come upon me, and that which I was afraid of is come unto me.

—Job 3:25

Water the daisies.
    Watch the dirt   turn dark
        with relief.

Love the bees. Like you, they have
      names and middle names,
memories,   deaths.

Open your hand
      to the tug and huff
of toddlers,   the macaroni on the table
      hardened to half-smiles,   half-moons.

Watch the fish rise
         from the lake   of childhood.
See how they're filled   ·   by the fruit of air.

Refine stillness. Let the good milk spill.

Praise each freckle,
    a star   in a constellation
        of your vast   fleshy galaxy.

Thank it—
    what eats your heart
into grave simplicity,   leaving it
easy to pack,   the pit of a plum.

Guard your true promise. Be lucid
and wide. Animal-soft.   Full as a bride.

What matters is nearly
         invisible.   Search for it
snout-like,   close to the ground,
      bloodhound sharp
                    and howl.

ACKNOWLEDGMENTS

Many thanks to the journals and magazines who first published these poems:

The Adirondack Review: "Poem After Ravel's *Daphnis et Chloé: Lent (chiffre 156) Peu à Peu*"

Coal Hill Review: "Envy"

Cutthroat: A Journal of the Arts: "The Way Things Are Going in Liberty, Utah"

Hunger Mountain Review: "Grief Sestina"

JuxtaProse: "Canning Tomatoes, Late August" and "Conversations with the Dead"

The Maynard: "The Year We Considered Foster Care"

Missouri Review: "Blackberry Jam"

Mom Egg Review: "Ghost"

New Ohio Review: "Rodeo" and "What We Did at the End of the World"

On the Seawall: "We Drew Out the Feeble Language"

Pratik: "Self-Portrait at Twelve"

Ruminate: "April 23, 2020, and Today Is Shakespeare's Birthday" and "When It Comes"

Small Orange Journal: "Jenny's Slot Canyon, Evening, Late November"

Sugar House Review: "Everywhere I Look I See a Rodeo" and "I Drive Past the Cemetery"

SWWIM: "So Long"

Terrain.org: "Ode to the Skunk Who Lives in the Woodpile I Pass on My Morning Walk" (originally published as "For the Skunk Who Lives in the Woodpile I Pass on My Morning Walk") and "Teapot Lake on the Head of a Pin"

West Trestle Review: "Letter to Josie Bassett Morris"

The Westchester Review: "Buddha Has Returned"

Western Humanities Review: "Don't Feed the Coyotes"

Whale Road Review: "Alaskan Abecedarian"

ꙮ

"Valentine for the Great Salt Lake" is part of *irreplaceable, a collective praise poem for Great Salt Lake* curated by Nan Seymour and published by Moon in the Rye Press.

"Rodeo" won the inaugural NORward Poetry Prize from *New Ohio Review.*

"The Way Things Are Going in Liberty, Utah" won the Joy Harjo Prize from *Cutthroat: A Journal of the Arts.*

"Grief Sestina" was runner-up for the Ruth Stone Poetry Prize from *Hunger Mountain Review*.

"Ghost" was a finalist for the Nina Riggs Poetry Award from *Cave Wall*.

Many of these poems were included in my chapbook *The Ache and the Wing* (winner of the Sundress Chapbook Contest, Sundress Publications, 2021).

◡

A ginormous thank you to my poetry group, Laura Stott and Natalie Taylor, whose deadlines and suggestions helped this book come into being and whose own experiences of child loss have comforted me and kept me company when I needed it most.

Humbled thanks to the legendary Patricia Smith for selecting *Rodeo* for The Donald Justice Poetry Prize. I told you it would change my life. Meeting you was a big part of that.

Thanks to the community of poets and writers who I have the great privilege to know and work with. A writing life is a good life.

Sincerest thanks to Christine Stroud, Mike Good, and the team at Autumn House Press. Working with you has been a dream come true.

Thank you—again!—to Kristin Carver for your gorgeous original art that graces the covers of each of my books. You inspire me.

Love and thanks to my parents, David and Kathy Brown and Teri and Craig Karren, and to my in-laws, Blake and Jolene Wilkinson, for their constant support. And to my entire family.

Deepest thanks to Sean, Cael, Beck, and Cooper, whose love and light inspire these poems. Strawberries and fire. And to Jude, for your brief but luminous presence. We miss you.

And thanks to my God, the companion of my life.

NOTES

"Rodeo" refers to the Ogden Pioneer Days Rodeo, an annual, week-long rodeo that celebrates the settling of Utah by the Mormon Pioneers.

"Self-Portrait at Twelve" is an imitation of the poem "Self-Portrait" by Kiki Petrosino, the first poem in her excellent poetry collection *Witch Wife*.

"Someday Soon" takes its title from a song of the same name, written by Ian Tyson. I grew up listening to the version recorded by Judy Collins, an artist who has had a profound influence on my life and art.

"I Drive Past the Cemetery" quotes lines from Van Morrison's "Sweet Thing" and refers to "My Sweet Lord" by George Harrison.

"Ring" refers to the Ring of Fire Solar Eclipse of October 2023, which my family watched from Bryce Canyon National Park.

Many of these poems are rooted in place, and I acknowledge the power and influence in my life of wild spaces, including southeastern Alaska, the Sonoran Desert, and my beloved home, high desert Utah, which includes the Wasatch and Uinta Mountains, the Great Salt Lake, and the myriad slot canyons, valleys, and trails that have inspired these poems.

DONALD JUSTICE POETRY PRIZE

The West Chester University Poetry Center welcomes submissions of unpublished, original book-length manuscripts that pay attention to form for consideration in this competition.

Since 2018, Autumn House Press has published the Donald Justice Poetry Prize-winning manuscript. The Donald Justice Poetry Prize is part of the Spencer Poetry Awards at West Chester University.

The following list indicates the winner as well as the judge:

2023: *Ghost Man on Second* by Erica Reid, selected by Mark Jarman

2022: *The Scorpion's Question Mark* by J. D. Debris, selected by Cornelius Eady

2021: *Out of Order* by Alexis Sears, selected by Quincy R. Lehr

2020: *No One Leaves the World Unhurt* by John Foy, selected by J. Allyn Rosser

2019: *Voice Message* by Katherine Barrett Swett, selected by Erica Dawson

2018: *The Last Visit* by Chad Abushanab, selected by Jericho Brown

NEW AND FORTHCOMING
FROM AUTUMN HOUSE PRESS

I Have Not Considered Consequences: Short Stories by Sherrie Flick

The Worried Well by Anthony Immergluck
Winner of the 2024 Rising Writer Prize, selected by Eduardo C. Corral

Bigger: Essays by Ren Cedar Fuller
Winner of the 2024 Autumn House Nonfiction Prize, selected by Clifford
    Thompson

The Great Grown-Up Game of Make-Believe by Lauren D. Woods
Winner of the 2024 Autumn House Fiction Prize, selected by Kristen Arnett

self-driving by Betsy Fagin
Winner of the 2024 Autumn House Poetry Prize, selected by Kazim Ali